Angel Wings & Heart Strings

SHARON M. KIRKPATRICK

Copyright © 2020 by Sharon M. Kirkpatrick.

ISBN   Softcover   978-1-951469-35-1

All rights reserved. No part of this book may be reproduced or transmitted in any form or by any means, electronic or mechanical, including photocopying, recording, or by any information storage and retrieval system without express written permission from the author, except in the case of brief quotations embodied in critical reviews and certain other non-commercial uses permitted by copyright law.

Printed in the United States of America.

To order additional copies of this book, contact:
Bookwhip
1-855-339-3589
www.bookwhip.com

Contents

POEMS OF LOVE

What Will Be Will Be	11
Angels in Flight	13
Angels Touch	14
Lost Love	15
Doves in Flight	16
Say I Love You	17
Angelic Love In Vain	18
My Special Earth Angel	19
I Will Always Love You	20
Brother	21
My Child's Laughter	22
My Son's Love	23
Brother's Love	24
Brother Dear	25
My Beloved Sister	26
In My Dreams	27
A Bit of Hope	28
Above The Mist	29
Love is in the Air	30
Be There	31
Friends	32
Till the End of Time	33
Be With Me This Night	34
Our Unforgotten Love	35
Soul to Keep	36
Just Like You	37
Angel Once Mine	38
Tonight	39
Time	40
Angel Wings	41
Belong	42
"The One" Who Never Let Go	43

Dreams of Enchantment	44
I Could	45
Still	46
Soul of My Seed	47
I Feel Love	48
Now Until Eternity	49
Have No Fear	50
Could I Have Said I Love You	51
Memories of Days Gone By	52
One of a Kind	53
Cowboys in Disguise	54
Fulfilled	55
Carrousel by the Sea	56
Until Eternity	57
Turn Around	58
Angels Tears	59
Bird in a Gilded Cage	60
Wedding Day Blessing	61
Completion	62
Christmas Time	63
Indian Love Song	64
Angel in My Room	65
Soul Mate	66
Our First Dance	67
Souls On Fire	68
You The Angels And Me	69
You	70
Believe in Love	71
The Angels Are Coming	72
Fallen Angels	73
Impossible	74
Finally	75
You Are the One	76
Dreams Can Come True	77
Destiny	78
I Am Loved	79

INSPIRATION AND PROPHECY

Love of God 83
Time and Prophecy 84
The King and I 85
Peace 86
The Great Gathering 87
Dreams of Paradise 88
Calling of the Great Spirit 89
Redeemed 90
Chancellors of Hope 91
Stargate 77 92
Feeble Hearts 93
Hand in Hand 94
Dreams Concealed 95
Defying Destiny 96
Thanks 97
Tomorrow 98
New Dawn 99
Time is Near 100
Farwell 101
Heaven's Gate 102
Falling Star 103
Rein in Peace 105
Our Descent 106
Are You Ready 107
Out of the Chill 108
Time is Soon At Hand 109
Angels of Light 110
Love 111
Satan Lets Go 112
Open Door 113
Battles Won 114
Last Call 115
Wind Song 116
Victory Across the Land 117
I Am Jesus 118

Dedication

I would like to give special thanks to Jesus Christ who has always been my inspiration to write this poetry. Without him in my life, this book would not have been possible. All the trials and situations I have been placed in to experience love, loss, disappointment in mankind, and love, was what brought about the deep feelings from my heart, knowing that the choices that we make in life can render a lot of pain, growth and happiness. Until you place your life in the Lords hands and follow his guidance, will you discover real love and discover life the way it was meant to be lived. The deep seeded messages in *Angel Wings and Heartstrings* could have only been expressed through his guidance.

I would also like to thank all of you that played a role in my life, because without you, the book would not have been possible.

To my parents for standing behind me whenever I fell and encouraging me to get up and keep going and encouraging me to continue to write more poetry.

To my husband who is my best friend, who continues to teach me every day and has encouraged me to publish this book.

To my children who have walked every step of the way with me and never lost hope.

I would also like to give a special thanks to my doctors, Dr. Heidinger in Klamath Falls, Oregon and Dr. Stuart in Bend, Oregon for making sure that my needs are met because of the chronic pain I deal with daily. Without their help I couldn't have gone on. I also thank Dr. Heidinger for standing up and being a witness for the Lord in his practice by having a Christian practice. I feel that he also has been encouragement for me to stand up for Jesus in my book with the hope that I may touch many people's hearts and bring them back to the Lord.

Poems of Love

What Will Be Will Be

Last night I had a dream
of things yet unforeseen
of hearts full of doubt
of feelings of being without
I find myself in a ship at a wedding
the people so in love
I started to gaze at the heavens above
my desire to have you there
this precious moment to share
all of a sudden a white object in the sky appeared
I felt it was the beginning of the end, I feared
awesome sights of other planets coming into view
I rushed to see if I could find you
with desperation I spun you around
and said, I have something to say
time is short, it must be said today
with tears in our eyes
we quickly learned of love and compromise
in one flashing moment, our whole lives before us
we turned all our doubt into trust
I said, get ready my love
watch the signs from above
timing is everything
watch the signs of Spring
watch the water rise
watch for new signs in the skies
of radiant unseen bright lights
the world and us rapidly reaching greater heights
all I know at this moment, what I feel for you is real
there is no longer time for me to conceal
so, I will say to you today
you must trust what you see is real along the way
let it be known
how very close our souls have grown
we have not taken this journey alone
yet there is a sadness and regret

for all the time we have not spent
will there be time for you and me
all I know, what will be will be.

Angels in Flight

Transpiring angel in my life
keeping me warm all throughout the night
touching my heart and healing every part
with her peaceful loving arms
that lift me up and keep me from all harm
delightful celestial sounds
that let me know you will always be around
with gentle waves of love so deep
I pray her soul to keep
such beautiful heavenly love
my soul feels as though it has wings to fly like the doves
answers come to be
answers that set me free
no more good-byes
no more asking why
just two hearts that beat as one
sharing love so deep and warming
from even tide until morning sun

Angels Touch

Have you ever been touched by an angel
or gazed into her eyes
if you allow her
she will take you from here to paradise
soft swirling motions around you flow
so gently given before you realize or know
she offers purity and light
stop and accept if you think you might
touching me warmly when I am falling apart she reaches into the
depths of my heart
in the deepest darkness of the night
comes the memories of her piercing light
like a beacon she guides me through
to a brighter tomorrow and skies of blue
each day that I awake
my guiding angels path I will take
I do no require much
only my angels touch.

Lost Love

Our love had just begun
why did you decide to run
you were becoming my life
I wanted to make you my wife
now I sit here waiting for your beckon call
while watching my lonely teardrops fall
your spirit feels as though it is present, yet you are so far away
come back to me, I love you and have so much more to say
I have been desperately searching for your precious love
but it is nowhere to be found
I pray to the universe and to God above
he will bring you back to me, my lost love.

Doves in Flight

Beautiful doves coo in the night
as they see our souls take wings in flight
harmonizing as we sing
thanking God for everything
rising above the skies so blue
healing the earth, blessing the flowers we grew
one day I knew I would find
my soul mate, my final destiny
come fly with me day and night
joined as one, as doves in flight.

Say I Love You

Love is a once in a lifetime thing
you'll know because your heart will start to sing
glistening eyes and those special glances
that often catch you by surprise
and when you touch, starts the wanting sighs
take time each day
never let emotions get in the way
of saying I love you
you know it will be accepted
because we never know how long love will stay
say I love you before it is too late and time has passed
a sweet smile will cross over their heart
even though they are near or far apart
a remembrance of that sweet little refrain
will touch them like the smell of sweet roses
after freshly fallen rain
after years have passed with a quick look back
they will think, I remember you, you always said I love you
now without you near, I remember how special and dear, you
always said I love you.

Angelic Love In Vain

Love to an angel given in vain
is felt with so much remorse and pain
I did try to tell you I loved you so
only then to watch you go
once again my heart is loc.ked away
not knowing if it will open again someday
the flaming light of love is slowly burning out
with unexpected waves of emptiness and doubt
an angel never really knows if she will meet that special one
or drift from sun to setting sun
memories of a rushing fire
are all that is left of her loving desire
if your heart you should ever meet
I pray her love you will honorably keep
embedded deep within my mind
are precious moments of those special times
Gods speed be with my angel love
may the blessings be yours from heaven above
and may your angelic love never be taken in vain.

My Special Earth Angel

Only angels walk in her presence
love abides all around her essence
her love is so astounding
she will never know
how I loved her so
she flows with the wind
heavenly chimes, oh how they ring
when a new love she doth begin
so taken with their love is she
and when it vanishes she says
with tears, tis time to leave
she parts with such sweet love and sorrow
in hopes for a brighter day tomorrow
grant her the love she is so deserving of
lift her heart and wings to fly free as a dove
let her know, let her know it is me
for in love with her I fell
she will always be my special earth angel.

I Will Always Love You

I have wondered why it could not be
why you could not have been closer to me
but through the air waves
our love still remains the same
I cherish pleasant memories
that is all I ever had
when I think of you mom and dad though there have been times I know
your hearts were filled with endless doubt and woe
just remember your little angel is still at work becoming whole
you gave me wings to fly
sometimes questioning and wondering why
truly someday you will see
your daughter shining in pure ecstasy
a heart so full of love
though her wings are tattered and torn
she has won, she has ridden out the storm
with my deepest appreciation I send
thankfulness without end
bless you both, your hearts and souls
think of the beach and of me
that is when you set my soul free
I hope that when you look back
you will say I am pleased, not sad
I will always love you mom and dad.

Brother

When I am lost and feel I have gone astray
you are always there come what may
though you are just a stranger
who sometimes calls in the middle of the night
you are such a friend
I think we might just know each other
like a long lost sister and brother
thanks for being there, showing me that you care
like a special messenger from a far distant plain
sending your love through the airwaves
I am pleased that I have finally discovered
that indeed we truly are all sisters and brothers.

My Child's Laughter

The sweetest day came for me
when I opened my eyes to see
this beautiful child laying in my arms
so delicate and beautiful the light that surrounded her
so blessed I felt to have given birth
to this blessing from heaven
as time went by
I wanted only to protect her with my life
then came the hard times and teen years
with all its little mysteries and fears
of losing her somehow
throughout it all she taught me how to laugh and smile
now that you are a grown woman
with a family of your own
life just keeps getting better
and for all of this I give thanks to my beautiful daughter
I know I can be at peace
that life cannot take from me
the miracle of life and my child's laughter.

My Son's Love

As with the breaking of a new dawn
I awoke to find I had been blessed with a son
a new feeling flowed through me like a song
this heavenly baby full of innocence and love
so remarkable was this little boy
filling my home with so much joy
at times there were little troubles that came about
yet in my heart he brought peace with little room for doubt
that he would grow to be
the wonderful man standing in front of me
on this his wedding day
so full of love, is he
so refined, handsome and gallant
I couldn't be more proud and so astounded
that God blessed me with my sons love.

Brother's Love

Looking back I sure can remember
only the greatest of times
my big brother teaching me what trees to climb
what doll was best to play with, Bob or Jim
how you always seemed to be there when life got dim
I hope you will always remember the happy days of our lives
memories are what keep the ties
somehow I have always known
you would show me the way though far from home
so no matter what roads we seek
my love for you in my heart I will always keep
for there is nothing more precious or special that I know of
than my brother's love.

Brother Dear

I have shed many a tear
for the lost and broken years
I think of times
when we were at play
I remember them as though they were yesterday
at times I have thought
has my brother forgotten me
or too wrapped up in life that he could not see
where is my little sister
torn by her path in life though she is so dear
I pray in days to come
the good memories will far succumb
that one day we can be
walking hand in hand, you and me
as if to say
I will always love you come what may
for in my heart
my love still reverenced and so sincere
that I can still say I love you brother dear.

My Beloved Sister

Oh, sister, my sweet sister have no fear
though I am far away I am always near
dare you take the time
to remember happy days we had in our lives
memories are what makes us grow
look back and you will know
that through it all
what we have become through all our falls
remember the laughs and the fun we had
and now life doesn't seem so bad
as time rolls on, do not be bitter
for you will always be
my beloved sister.

In My Dreams

You come to me in the night
and dance and hold me tight
a light of love shines all around
as you say your love just cannot be found
the intensity of your love
I know must be sent from heaven above
I dream of passion and of love ever given
as you come to me and I ask will I ever be forgiven
oh, my dear precious soul
do you not realize or know
when we are together, two halves make a whole
you come to me with such feeling of desire
touching my soul, sending it higher and higher
as the dream ends you hold out your hands and say
I have been waiting for you for a long time, please stay
as the dawn breaks and I awake to find you gone
once again tonight I will play your love song
hoping as the angels sing
I will again touch and hold you in my dreams.

A Bit of Hope

Here is a secret you cannot keep
that when you look in your heart
you will find me
even as you sleep
who am I and what do I seek
I am the keeper of your heart
lasting love eternally deep
like a moth to a flame
God drew you to me
and I alone could set your soul free
what is life without love
two souls gentle as t he doves
can finally break free
from all earthly bounds
flying free to higher ground
so if with life you cannot cope
I will be there to share this little bit of hope.

Above The Mist

Above the mist, down through the clouds
comes my angel without a sound
bringing love into my room
my whole attention doth she consume
she lingers with such delight
giving messages of love deep into the night
other entities tempt me, but I sustain
I want only her love to remain
when the morning dew lies on the ground
I wonder where can my angel love be found
my soul calls out that she is missed
knowing tonight we will join once more above the mist.

Love is in the Air

Love is in the air
you can feel it calling everywhere
I will follow love to the ends of the earth
for it is a brilliant and shining ember
you can see day and night
showing our hearts will not always be in decline
on the wings of love we will embark
now that I have found you
we will make love everlasting in our hearts
sparkling glances in the night
fulfilled wishes and promises of delight
days filled with the fragrance of flowers
a beautiful scent filling the air from our window bowers
what, you ask do you mean to me
your love and devotion are my everything
gentle touches, whispered kisses,
enwrapped with romantic candlelight
fulfill my fondest wishes as we hold each other tight
I thank God for answered prayer
you are here and
love is in the air.

Be There

I think of you with one last prayer
that you will think of me when I am not there
fond memories are recaptured
from days spent, already gone by
touch my heart and heal my soul
tell me your love will never go
when I look into your eyes
they gleam with such love to my surprise
just knowing, truly knowing
I have found
a love so lasting and beautifully profound
now I am assured that our love is one of a kind
that our souls are eternally entwined
it is my last prayer, you sent by God
will always be there.

Friends

Some friends squander you away
some keep you at bay
others send flowers
in your darkest 'hours
real friends hold true
through your deepest sorrows
and in your brighter tomorrows
friendship outweighs the test of time
and is never ever unkind
real friends love unconditionally
so you can let go to fly free
with all the ebb and flow
they always hold true yet seem to know
the right things to say and do
tell me what you know
will you be friend or foe
do you see the friend you have found in me
that I will not fail to see
the truth
of what it means to be friends.

Till the End of Time

When I met you on one starry night
the pieces fit, everything felt right
could it be
God created you just for me
as time goes on
I think of you from dusk till dawn
once again I have learned how to smile
once again I want you for more than just a while
candlelit evenings
and long walks on the beach
I miss you when you are out of reach
the time has come for me to say
love is here, truly here to stay
I want you to be mine
till the end of time.

Be With Me This Night

Come be with me this night
for you are my only light
when I see your sweet precious smile
I feel like walking that extra mile
when you wrap your loving arms around me so tight
my heart is filled with so much joy and delight
you make me laugh and you tickle me
you always know what to say to me
there have been times I have felt alone
but only when you start to roam
when can I keep you just for me
can you not see, we were meant to be
I want to be consumed by the goodness of your soul
oh, my love, I would give you my all
what a beautiful day it would be
when we unite in perfect harmony
soon it will be our time
until then,
be with me this night.

Our Unforgotten Love

Can I see you tonight
or do I give up this fight
does absence really make the heart grow fonder
or leave room for doubt as my mind starts to ponder
are you really there
do you really care
you say there is no one else
no room for anyone but myself
you say there is so much to do
that does not include you
gifts of love I bring
hoping someday you will remember one thing
from the very start
I could have given you my heart
I guess I wouldn't if I were smart
remember the beauty of loves essence
while in each other's presence
no one could touch us then
only one day to see it all end
messages from God of future days
are fitting together
I am no longer in a haze
so re-define, what is love
I need to believe
that with love our souls can retrieve
before time is at an end
will we try it over again
touch me now before I go
let your feelings start to show
remembering somewhere in time
you were truly mine
as sure as I know there is a heaven above
I know we will meet again to complete
our unforgotten love.

Soul to Keep

So here we are
two souls together from two distant stars
they said some day we would meet
that we would feel alive and so complete
look at the Spring
now I see the beauty in everything
listen to the sweet music
each sound so intensified
feel the love, we are quenched and satisfied
as we soar above the clouds
a vision of you is all I had to hold until now
others had tried my soul to keep
but my love for you was longing and deep
now you are here
reaching beyond once thought impossible dreams
are coming true, because of you it seems
when I am in my deepest sleep
you assure me
I have your soul to keep.

Just Like You

Wait my precious angel
please don't be so blue
for I am out here waiting, looking for you
I long to hear your voice
for you are my only choice
in God's love I do trust
that he alone knows what is best for us
someday our love will begin
we will know love without limits
I am waiting for you
angel with a heart so true
I know this for I am just like you

Angel Once Mine

Oh angel, my sweet angel
looking for the promise of love
am I really your chosen one
although I have tried
my thoughts and actions speak of lies
you know and so you run
hoping tomorrow will bring your special one
somehow deep down inside
all these feelings I cannot hide
a little love here
a little love there
not enough for a treasure so rare
oh angel, my sweet angel
I felt closer to love than ever before
could I afford to have given you more
her heart once open, is now is closed
oh angel, my sweet angel
what damage have I spun
can it ever be undone
all I can do is hope in time
you will return to me
angel once mine.

Tonight

Tonight, tonight, you will be with me
from now until eternity
I will love you with all my heart
as I have from the very start
you will be mine as I am yours
as heaven opens its pearly doors
to see me say to you
I have waited for you for a long time
now you are in my arms
You are love, you are mine
tonight.

Time

Time, what is time
give me your love, and I'll give you mine
you have waited, your heart remains so true
I can only go from day to day in hope that I will find you
you are the purest soul I have ever known
pure enough to weather any storm
now take my heart and take my soul
again as one we can will go
to do Gods work upon this land
together, united we stand
with love lasting and true
I knew God would bring me to you
time, what is time.

Angel Wings

Wrapped so tightly within my angels wings
as she utters promises of hope for lost dreams
she will pull at my heart, urging me to let go
binding me with love down to my very soul
healing all memories, as I dream of pain
she cleanses me while I stand in the falling rain
showing me hope for future days
saying you are never alone
there will always be hope
walking hand in hand
so I don't fall
in weak and shifting sand
with rays of sunlight around her sweep
drying my tears she sings her music pure and sweet
as I slumber, as I sleep
I am secure and at peace
wrapped within my angels wings.

Belong

Why did you not see
the deepest part of her soul
henceforth, come orders from God
it is time to go
so on her journey she went
time with you is now spent
apart in a world of gloom
suddenly, like a flower coming into bloom
the hard times have passed and the pain is at an end
a new love awaits around the bend
watch carefully and lend an ear
the angels are singing
as your angel disappears
tonight, as you lay in that sullen bed
think of all the things you could have done or said
how could you have been so wrong
it is of no matter now, God has closed the door
she doesn't belong to you anymore
to another her love is strong
to another she now belongs.

"The One" Who Never Let Go

The brilliant stars that once shone bright
are all gone and out of sight
now, I am feeling lost in this lonely bed
as dreams of you fill up my head
I am once again free
my heart rests peacefully
dreams are all that is left you see
I pray that they will never be taken from me
come down and join me now
in your presence I will whole heartedly bow
give me back our sweet time
reach out and you will find
the real me you sought to know
"the one" who never let go.

Dreams of Enchantment

Oh my love
my true love
I have waited forever
now you're here
have no fear
I will always be with you
one more time
true love we find
lasting memories that bind
take my heart and take my soul
as blossomed memories unfold.
(Taken from a dream with the melody of Braham's Lullaby).

I Could

I could want you
but only with mine eyes
I could taste you
but there would be no spice
I could need you
but only go insane
I could miss you
but that would bring no change
I could run from you
but my heart still knows the truth
I could say I am hurt by you
but then you'd know I am blue
I could fantasize about you
but without you, what is the point
I can stay clear of you
but I would only go further into myself
I could urge you forward
but I am not sure you would come
I could convince you to stay where you are
but then we would grow further apart
I could tell you I love you
but to my heart I must hold true
I could go on forever not knowing
but the pain would just keep growing
I could ask you to look at me
but I am afraid you might see
I could tip at anytime
but I would be totally out of my mind
I would not fail for you, even if I could.

Still

Instant beauty
that is what I see in thee
you have opened my eyes
to hidden mysteries I have kept inside
in past times you showed me how
to look beyond the clouds
here I sit high on this mountain top
flying in my mind into the valleys I drop
ever so gently now
leaping forward from bow to bow
as I remember what you said to me
all you can do is be the best you can be
for life has just begun
as you walk beside me
from sun till setting sun
dance with me now my angel and feel
how deep my love has grown for you so real
for you are the amulet of light
and forever will always shine bright
in this tattered heart of mine
leading me back somewhere in time
where all I knew was pure sweet love
walk with me again this night
and let your ambress colors of blue shine ever bright
healing my heart from all the emptiness I have known
knowing you are "the one" and how our love has grown
please allow me to say
as one with God's love we will always stay
and you are with me still.

Soul of My Seed

Time loss means a lot
are there memories we have forgot
our lives have seen so many twists and turns
yet it is love that our souls still urn
are we still able to recognize the signs
or will we stay so busy that love passes us by
now that I am at my journeys send
I think of you and ask why did we come to an end
why do I feel so bound
my spirit lost not sure it can be found
oh, my love if I had only taken the time
to love you, you would still be mine
I am sorry I did not see
the love for you hidden deep inside of me
now you are gone
to another you belong
how can I say what is forever captured in my heart and soul
given the time we could have become one and so perfectly whole
so now as I face the future, only to see
the love lost between you and me
tears fill up my eyes
I search for your love and find no compromise
I want to come to you with my heart so open and true
till then I pray the angels will hold the love for me deep within you
give us a chance to share a lifetime of memories of past and present true
I say to you now as you stand before me
I deeply, truly love you, I have no more needs
just you my angel, soul of my seed.

I Feel Love

I feel love
I feel love
happiness is regained
new life is now sustained
it seems like lifetimes have gone by
since last I gazed into your eyes
the current storms have all passed
and now your love is here at last
I feel love
I feel love
why did I ever fear
I would find your love so sincere
love that will grow from year to year
now I sing from the mountain tops
you are here and I feel love.

Now Until Eternity

It started with a glance
as you asked me to dance
uncontrolled passion flew from our eyes
of familiar unforgotten ties
and as our bodies touched
with one electrifying kiss
lead to another one of bliss
listen to our hearts pounding in time
as we danced not scared of what we could find
if we have really found
the love we searched for without bounds
do we forget this memorable night
and the loving light we see in each other's eyes
or should we let this love flow
into pure nothingness as endless love unfolds
I knew there would come a time
when I would find
my one true love
whom I have searched for many, many years
through so many disappointments and tears
please walk with me
from now until eternity.

Have No Fear

How sweet it is
this life I miss
for I am on the other side
but my feelings I cannot hide
someday out of the blue
I will step down from my clouds
to find you
I know you have tried for so very long
to be trusted, true and strong
the vow we made from past life
will begin again my sweet wife
you will see me again
our life will begin anew until the end
keep your light shining my precious star
I will find you no matter how near or far
with God all things are possible
hold your heart for me my dear
I will soon be with you have no fear.

Could I Have Said I Love You

Grasping at the last ray of light
knowing I will once more be alone tonight
why could I not say
I love
chances are
do you wish on that same bright star
I wonder where you could be
I wish you were right here next to me
please come back, come back and stay
I will do all the things I did not do yesterday
If you were to come back to stay
I love you would thrust from my lips
I would say it over and over to prove I meant it
I dream endlessly of what I would do
I would be holding you, caressing you, never letting you go
please take away my sorrow
give me a brighter day tomorrow
if you could only know the truth
I could have said I love you.

Memories of Days Gone By

Bring tome
those precious memories
of days gone by
when we felt so high, that we could touch the sky
moments of ecstasy
is what I felt when you were next to me
time and space could never erase
the love I saw written on your face
our love was a work of art
I felt it begin from the very start
for with you, two halves made a whole
we could see through each other's soul
how many years ago that was
though it seems like yesterday, as I sigh
as I treasure those memories of days gone by.

One of a Kind

Angels are hard to find and believe me
are one of a kind
so if you should find a soul so dear
hold her in your arms ever near
with her you cannot fail
she will be your dreams in detail
she will love your very soul
until you feel fulfilled and completely whole
if an angel you should ever meet
you will love her ways and love her deep
she will lift your soul to higher ground
and when you are in doubt her love will stay sound
she will spread wings of love around you every night
wings wrapped holding you tight
you will always feel safe
with unconditional love that will always remain
stay with me and this heart of mine
for I have found angels are hard to find
and one of a kind.

Cowboys in Disguise

Riding across cobalt blue midnight skies
then suddenly the day arrives
into this world we are thrown
wondering through this life alone
trudging through deep winter snow
wrestling cattle as the hot and sandy winds blow
horses become our friends and masters
they teach us to look within
learning to keep only to ourselves in a world full of sin
riding into the sunset, mountains so high
hoping once again to reach those cobalt blue midnight skies
across the golden meadows the wind whispers songs of peace
what more could a cowboy really need
a cowboys life is not so bad
learning to tune into nature, be one with the animals, but still
in search of the life we once had
God brought us here, now knowing the reason
to spread love and peace throughout each and every season
I have found my souls release
when I think of God who is never out of reach
now, I look at the midnight sky and realize
that some cowboys are really angels in disguise.
(dedicated to Jim Morrison)

Fulfilled

My heart starts to sing
because of you
and the love that you bring
I have so much joy
no one can destroy
my life can now burst forth
my feet do not even touch the earth
you have shown me so much
with just one look, one touch
I can never deny
the love I have held for you deep inside
how beautiful the day will be
when you are standing next to me
all the angels will sing
the day of our wedding
the love that we will feel
we will be completely fulfilled.

Carrousel by the Sea

At seventeen I stepped on the carrousel of life
to my surprise, what did I find
my very first love holding the brass ring
saying, I am yours for the taking
so, around and around we would go
until the carrousel came down to a slow
I got off and chose another horse to ride
keeping all my excitement locked inside
I didn't stop until every horse I chose
except for the last one with a painted rose
somehow, I was afraid to climb on
for it was you see
the closest to the brass ring
then all of a sudden
the carrousel stopped
and I got off
I found myself not a child any longer
but, the memory of that one horse
kept getting stronger and stronger
so, I searched for that old carrousel
until one day, I found it, what a miracle
and on the last horse was a man
he said, jump on
as fast as you can
we both grabbed for that old brass ring
we got it, amazingly
I realized that this man was different
one that I could keep
so happy and content were we
watching our children on the carrousel by the sea

Sharon M. Kirkpatrick

Until Eternity

Let it be me you spend your time with
I feel blessed with such a wonderful gift
if I had only known from the very start
I could have trusted you with my heart
you have given me time
the wasted years are in decline
all the endless doubts and fears
that have been there for years
I can now release and let go
now that you have come along
I am filled with such beautiful song
only peace and tranquility
in your eyes do I see
all I ask is that you never change
that I will finally be able to exchange
the love I have saved deep inside of me
from now until eternity.

Turn Around

In the solitude of my thoughts
think of loneliness and what it has taught
my tears flow from the depths of my heart
filling my empty soul every part
although I have tried to fill it with
endless roads and dreams
somehow without love I am lost, so it seems
untrue lovers and careless days
nights go on forever, dreams left in a haze
I plunge into other things
hoping to place some meaning to life
yet no matter what I do
a promise of happiness never comes true
are there any truths to this world at all
I wonder each and every nightfall
friends, children and lovers gone their way
please dear God, not another lonely day
then comes the morning, what will I do
fight off old memories in search of some happiness to pursue
there seems to be less and less time
no more dreams left to unwind
I had always hoped my true love I would find
in my heart, no maybe it was just in my mind
as I turn the last page of this earthly life
once again I pray God will not disappoint me
that I will turn and there you will be
hands reached out asking, have you been searching for me
once again my heart will sing
looking at you as in my fondest dreams
God will send us his promised rainbows
as he says "keep the faith, never let go"
you are almost there
turn around, look, he is there.

Angels Tears

Oh angel, with a heart so dear
let me love you, have no fear
let me pierce through and watch you fall
let me be the one to say it is your last call
I will promise you diamonds and the purest of gold
and say I will be with you till my love runs cold
little did I realize
I would fall for you, losing my disguise
oh, what a game I started to play
I caused you so much unhappiness and pain
fear grips my very soul
the day I saw her go
I will never play this game again
because of the pain it has left within
from now, throughout all of my years
I will never forget my angels tears.

Bird in a Gilded Cage

A bird once caught, now free
there is no love lost between you and me
so with wings in flight I now go
thanking you for letting me fly ever so
gently amongst the stars
to the lands beyond Jupiter and Mars
no longer behind love lost bars
sweet music is all I hear
from my soul mate drawing near
no matter how near or how far
I will find my lucky star
how lucky that day for me
as love comes looking
for you see
freedom is love, not hate
I am no longer a bird in a gilded cage.

Wedding Day Blessing

Today you become one
joined to walk together sun after setting sun
your love is destined in time
low, there will not be a mountain you cannot climb
so beautifully entwined you shall be
surrounded by Gods light for the world to see
may the memory of this day bring joy, peace, happiness and love
may you be rich with blessings from the Lord above
when you see rainbows peak across your sky
as the years pass slowly by
it will be a reminder of your love joined on this your wedding day
the angels are rejoicing and will be sending
their very own wedding day blessings.

Completion

So this is it
by the impression I get
you have moved away
not much more left to say
something that started out to be so good
is now so misunderstood
our broken hearts are in decline
please God give me a sign
where did we go wrong
both of our hearts were so determined and strong
thinking nothing could tear us apart
but now here we are
the fighting has just gone too far
give us the strength to go on
if it is your will, I will move along
as his teacher I hope he will never forget
the lessons of our time spent
this love was heaven sent
we have taught each other much
remember the lessons
there is no more time
we have reached our completion.

Christmas Time

By Christmas time you will see
a new life opens for you and me
remember the colored bulbs so cheery and new
our souls will join as one as I marry you
so as we open our Christmas gifts
we thank our God for unconditional love to give
as the snow falls on this moonlit night
and I peer into familiar eyes
I have finally found the one I have searched for my whole life
I am thankful we will be sharing each and every Christmas time.

Indian Love Song

Many moons I have called for you
Night Hawk said you are coming
that we will walk many days by the sea
the day skies fill with purple hues
the rivers cry and sing love songs for you
by nightfall, I am alone within
the Great Spirit shows darkened shadows of you
till the sun rises again
how true can one soul be
but still I wait so patiently
come my love, come
think of how the Eagle and Dove fly
that is how we will be, you and I
let the Great White Spirit unite our hearts
to sing like the Meadow Larks
as streams join, flowing down the mountain
let us drink of each other's fountain
let time once again stand still
as it did in days gone by
let us be together as the sun, moon and sky
until then I must go on
to continue our Indian love song.

SHARON M. KIRKPATRICK

Angel in My Room

Angel in my room told me you were something
she said you would be just right for me
when we met
I knew you would be one I would not forget
angel in my room said walk with him for more than just a while
as I did my heart began to smile
angel in my room said don't give up
this man has had more than enough
angel in my room said show him all your love
you will blend closer then hand in glove
she said allow him to see all of you and maybe
you will find you were meant to be
through good times and bad
he will do the best he can
for there is so much love in his soul
in time you will know
this man is your destiny
one you will not have to leave
as I bid you farewell, I say thank you
for him, angel in my room.

Soul Mate

My heart does fly as free as the wind
when a new love begins
with your love I have learned
trusting, giving, loving everything
my heart has once more learned to sing
oops! There go my wings
spreading further than ever before
oops! There goes my heart, once closed
now an open door
I feel endless possibilities
when you are next to me
all this time
waiting, wondering where could you be
my soul was so very empty
what a beautiful surprise
the day I looked into your precious eyes
something familiar about you seemed to say, this is fate
let us walk together
my old friend, my soul mate.

Our First Dance

When I am awake
or when I am asleep
I pray the Lord my soul to keep
holy for the purest of love
I can hardly wait
till I reach those golden gates
to see your hands reached out
to welcome my love as before
even with my heart so torn
with such energy you draw me in
that I forget all my woes and past sins
the angels gather round as we dance
singing songs of this our new romance
old in some ways, but yet bran new
I am ingrained in past memories of you
so here we are
dancing underneath the heavenly stars
we have reached beyond time and space
assured that true, pure love can never be erased
let us walk across this beautiful land
let us dance our first dance.

Souls On Fire

Our souls are on fire
burning us with passion
taking us higher and higher
burning us with love .and delight
so much so, we never want to leave each other's sight
once desiring unconditional love, and finding none
bridges burned and promises that only came undone
until there was you
long awaited recognition of memories from the past
are finally coming true and are here at last
my only wish on this tender night
that two souls join as one in perfect flight
melodies of love now flow through
of beautiful lives lasting and true
proving for ever more
this is not a dream from some distant shore
two souls once lost are now found
two feet planted firmly on solid ground
wandering eyes searching for the one
at last find peace and new love has begun
with heart, body, mind and soul
we give thanks to God for two loving souls on fire.

You The Angels And Me

Here comes my bridegroom
standing beside me in this room
am I worthy of you
I feel not
of course you are
you are my bright and shining star
you have been tempted by others
but your heart stood firm, patient and true
the love of God guided you through
do you not feel
my love for you is real
look deep inside of your heart once more
let your bridegroom walk through your hearts door
soon it will be known across the land
you and I will walk hand in hand
Jet us go forth and do God's work
from now until eternity
you, the angels and me.

You

For so long I have been looking for you
when I gave up you appear out of the blue
bright blue glistening eyes
eyes I have dreamed of many times
is it true, could it be
you are the one, the one meant for me
all my dreams I thought were gone
now with renewed hope you come along
can I finally believe
or will my heart once more be deceived
tell me, oh tell me now
because inside is so much doubt
tell me you will do no harm
to my broken heart
make this love stay
for more than just one day
tell me long and tell me true
that it is you, finally you.

Believe in Love

Love left me high and dry
love left me alone to cry
love said there is no way
love said, believe come what may
love said here he is
in all his royalty and bliss
as meek and as gently as a lamb
reaching out his loving hands
saying, I want to marry you some day
love did find a way
love happened to me
love can happen to you
as sure as the heavens above
you must believe in love.

The Angels Are Coming

The angels are coming
to share this joyous event
hard earned dreams are coming true they said
the angels are coming
I am happy to say
we will be joined as one today
as in heaven, so below
all shall see a beautiful glow
a gift from the angels
of radiant love
when two souls are destined to be
today we will be joined in perfect harmony
as God sends his love to you and me
our guides smile down from heaven in peace
they wipe their tired brows and say
finally they will be married today
what a happy event this will be
because the angels are coming.

Fallen Angels

Angels from heaven have fallen
to save those who are calling
we can hear your faintest prayer
to give you strength and great repair
we are your teachers
as you are ours
you have experienced earth
with all its love, pain, death and rebirth
we are here to spread Gods healing light
to give new hope
when you are tired of the fight
we are the protectors to keep you from harm
to help you remember why you were born
into a world of sin
not to give in
we are here to remind you
of your path
with broken wings and lost halos
God is calling all his fallen angels.

Impossible

It is impossible to think
there was anyone like you
it is impossible to think
I could feel so much for you
it is impossible to ever imagine
life without you
it is impossible to give
my heart to someone new
it is impossible not to believe
the love we share is a rose in full bloom
it is not impossible to realize
how blessed we truly are
to have found what most would never find and call it impossible.

Finally

Almighty God, as powerful as you are
help me find my way to him
I haven't done so well thus far
I have watched love at my very feet
I have watched love's defeat you have given me strength
to endure this human race
be gentle my Lord
and gently awake
the love you placed within me
for I have hidden it away
and kept it at bay
because of the deceit I have found in others
there are those
that would try to steal your very soul
if you let them
guide my paths and show me the way
to find the one meant for me someday
when that day comes and I see his face
I will give you all my praise
because I trusted you
Finally.

You Are the One

Seems like forever till I found you
now, all my treasured dreams are coming true
all the love and happiness I had only dreamed of
are showing their colors with your rainbow showers of love
you give love to me so unconditionally
making my heart sing and my soul free
you send me endless thoughts I cannot forsake
my heart to keep, my soul to save
the enormous feelings of love I have held inside
now burst forth with so much pride
how beautiful this day for me
for today we become one, you and me
pearls, rings, satin, and lace
trailing ribbons fall from my slender shoulders as you unlace
and devour in love every part of my being
on this our honeymoon night, our beginning
me in love with you and you in love with me
Our new life has begun
You really are the one.

Dreams Can Come True

There are times life seems so sublime
there are times life's mountains we must climb
have patience and love will shine through
God has work for you and me to do
although the storm clouds do roll in
think of love and find me within
look deep in your heart
learn to trust, make a new start
accusations are all but words
if feeling of doubt around you whirl
your test is faith, you will endure
the master is still working with his plan
to unite us all till we get to the promise land
grasp onto life with all your might
believe you have wings
that will lift you in flight
forget your doubts, forget your fears
our fathers return is drawing near
heavenly messages will be sent to you
love is hope, and dreams can come true.

Destiny

You are my destiny
I knew you were for me
a love destined in time
a gift from the divine
love that gives hope
for all eternity
our souls are now safe and free
come with me my love
walk with me amongst the stars
I can tell you who you really are
you give me Gods peace
so my soul can finally release
this deep seeded love
planted there only by God
to share with only you
which is lasting and true
there will never come a time
I will not want you to be mine
You are my dream
You are my destiny.

I Am Loved

I am the child whose dreams you took away
I am the woman who loved unconditionally
I am the one who's trust you broke
I am the woman who one day awoke
to the reality
that it was time to leave
I am the woman who continued to try
I am the woman who learned it is not a good thing to cry
I am the woman in a gilded cage
trying to fly my wings, stopped with disappointment and dismay
I am the woman that one day broke loose
and realized I did not need an excuse
to live
I am the woman that has played every part to everyone
I am the woman that woke up and realized
that all is possible looking in the mirror through child like eyes
I am the woman who found her path
never again to look back
I am the woman who finally found love
and became one with God above
I am woman
I am loved.
(Dedicated to the Women's Crisis Center.)

Inspiration and Prophecy

Love of God

Angels come in many disguises
look deep and you will see the love in their eyes
many are the roads they've traveled
many have humbly fought your battles
for they have the purest intent you see
to love and care for everybody
when given the chance
and an angel should ask you to dance
take hold of her hand and don't let go
just feel the beauty of their very soul
if from an angel you must part
just think of the love left embedded in your heart
day and night you will feel them there
strengthening our hearts in need of great repair
once again you will open to the desire of love
and again believe in the love of God.

Time and Prophecy

It is time to move my children
to higher ground
to gather as many souls
as can be found
to make safe children
who will be lost
bring out all the love
that is in your hearts
listen to what is written amongst the stars
there is no more time to play
the day of reckoning is on its way
brief earthquakes are warning signs
time to go, it is time
take one deep breath and around you see
all the signs of Satan's iniquity
do not be fooled by lies you are told
the truth before your eyes will unfold
help those that are so in need
leave behind hearts of greed
yours will be a peaceful journey now
follow the guiding light as time allows
to find safety in fortresses of peace
to wait for Satan's release
his plan will be made clear
you will see
this is God's time and prophecy.

The King and I

The king and I
Sat talking one night
I asked, what is to be
for I cannot see
what do you want me to do
what is in front of me
doors open and doors close
I walk down road after road
am I on my life's chosen path
or do I still look to the past
to see what I have done
and where I have been
trying to conquer my sins
when is it time for me
when will my soul be free
have I done my best
will my soul ever find rest
you my friend find peace
only when you follow me
keep on your journey now
as God your father I vow
your happiest days are ahead
be ye not misled
you are one of my chosen one's
life for you has just begun
if it is happiness you pursue
look deep inside of you
many a challenge still lies ahead
do not take the easy road instead
go with the deepest desire of your heart
don't place yourself before others
know that love is the key to life
that's how we talk, the King and I.

Peace

I thought I heard his voice
amongst the most high
in the city of Israel
I saw the signs written in the sky
the battle of Armageddon
will soon be at hand
the walls were surrounded with the enemy
not an empty gate could you see
the people of Israel were not afraid
because God's army surrounded each gate
as Satan sounded his battle cry
but not one man stood u p on his side
into the gates of hell he was thrown for all eternity
now God's people can be at peace.

The Great Gathering

Now is the time
to join as one
now is the time
to follow the heavenly one's
funneled clouds of red and gray
mean great destruction
get on your way
what say yea
I say take heed
go where your heart says to go
feel from within and you will know
safe places for you and me
are far away from the roaring sea
angels of light will guide you on
leading you to safety protected from the storm
we are all gathering now, we the angels of light
we promise you are always within our sight
so when you feel the urgency to go
join with caravans of three seen on the road
you are the survivors sent to do your work
we have experienced your agony, but know your worth
in the last flickering moments you will see
why God has sent you and where to be
feelings of being distraught and being alone
you must keep pushing on till you are called home
when an opening in the clouds you see
you will know it is time for the great gathering.

Dreams of Paradise

The swells of Satan are rising high
as the day of redemption draweth nigh
heartache and sorrow will soar in every city
feelings of no more love, lost hope, and defeat
our children are lost with no place to go
while parents have such overloads
not enough money brings great concerns
feeling tired and overworked
all these troubles are Satan's plan
to destroy the people across the land
watch Satan as he tries
to usher in the Anti-Christ
we will be taken before that time
to that place called paradise
where we will witness the hand of God
sign, seal and deliver Satan and the evil ones
to the gates of hell for all eternity
while we and our Saviour will reign in peace
the time is drawing nigh
hold on to your dreams of paradise.

Calling of the Great Spirit

The Indians lived in this great country
long before the white man came
so enlightened with peace and knowledge were they
always to the Great Spirit they gave their praise
for the paradise they had found
worshipping the beauty of this worlds holy ground
then one day it all changed
all was taken and rearranged
little by little their land was taken
they felt they had been forsaken
great depression and total dismay
still live in their souls today
still praying to their maker above
to give them their freedom as has been long spoken of
as their anger builds from within
they will gather as the battle begins
to gain back the freedom they once knew
looking for new happiness to pursue
watch as the Great Spirit unfolds his plan
many hands will join across the land
looking forward to a better day
no longer will they be in captivity
we want our freedom and we want it now
to this we solemnly vow
once again peace will rein
once again there will be no pain
once again we shall be free
the way we have been taught it should be
be still and you will hear it
the calling of the Great Spirit.

Redeemed

The gates of hell are open wide
the grim reaper stands outside
waiting to take you in
to cause so much anguish and sin
darkness surrounds all of us night and day
while he tempts us to come his way
and though he has destroyed so many
on our path we must stay
do not be misled by his evil ways
remember the promises God has made
He will not allow you to fall
you must answer his last call
be yea not deceived
time is now to be redeemed
watch now for the last signs
rediscover what love is and why
the angels of light are drawing near
hoping your souls to recapture
take time each day
get on your knees and pray
ask for God's forgiveness
know he is there and does listen
pray for those who have been lost
save their souls at any cost
life is short as you can see
time is now to be redeemed.

Chancellors of Hope

In the stillness of the night
I struggled to clear my mind
I wanted to be guided back
to lost life so dear
from walking the wrong paths for years
I felt undeserving of Gods' love
I would never be forgiven for what I have done
all of a sudden I saw a bright light
I thought I was going to lose my sight
three angels appeared to say
we are here to help, be ye not afraid
we are the chancellors of hope
we are here to help you let go
of the sin that has kept you bound
so you can move to safer ground
trust is in motion here
your path has been made clear
thanks to God, I was set free
from all of life's iniquity
if with life you cannot cope
call upon the Chancellors of hope.

Stargate 77

Stargate 77 is based near heaven
we at Stargate tap into you innermost thoughts
to help you remember what Jesus taught
transversal lights
fill your skies every night
most of you miss us as we pass by
how we adore your planet and wish to help
before your planet begins to die
so little of you listen to words we speak
we whisper messages for you to keep
we ask that you open your eyes
so you can see us as we pass by
we have so much knowledge to share
to keep you from so much despair
glad tidings we send
we the angels of light
we are with you until the end
today shines a new ray of hope
we are here
we do care
love and light be yours from heaven
this is your first message from Stargate 77

Feeble Hearts

How embalmed this earth is with things of no matter
their hearts have grown cold
to the temptress their souls are sold
how weak and feeble minded they are
what can I say to the children of this earth
how unfortunate their curse
how I have tried
how many times I have cried
but I cannot change their ways
I must come in haste
to save those that are left who still love me
in their weakened state
oh, with such sorrow I must say
soon it will be the day
I will take my loved ones from here
and I will be forced to destroy this earth
I cannot express how sad I am
but must follow Gods command
there will be nothing left but a void
where once there was so much joy
listen my children and you will hear
the trumpet sound loud and clear
although sad but true
soon I will come and get what is left of you
who have followed the light
and fought a good fight
the life you have known is of no matter now
time of deliverance
watch for signs in the fall and winter clouds
in the twinkling of an eye
storm clouds will lift you to the sky
there you will find safety
for you will be
with your heavenly father and me
no more chasing in the dark for feeble hearts.

Hand in Hand

As a cold chill enters over the land
God changes all paths with one command
I knew not what I was doing
now, I know where I am going
streams of light pierce the earth
God has given us a chance to rebirth
from nation to nation
sea to sea
new found freedom
for you and me
united as one this day we stand
new hope, joy and peace regained across the land
all those who are evil
no longer remain
no more tears from our souls
fall like rain
for now it is clear in God we trust
a new warmth like the sun
will shine all around us
have patience and faith and you will endure
with God at the helm we can now be sure
we are heading for the promise land, hand in hand.

Dreams Concealed

Sad moments of grief have all passed
when I finally see you, at last
sparkling rainbows of red and blue
saying how much I love you
purple hues paint heavens' sky
love is twinkling in your eyes
I am standing at heavens' gate
for the day I wait
for you to be with me
to see how wonderful life can be
sanctuary, love, peace and time
will be forever yours and mine
this is what my love would say
if he could only speak to me today
till the day God calls me home
I will cherish my dreams concealed.

Defying Destiny

I am the sorcerer in the night
in the day I take wings in flight
to that the destiny of my day
as night falls, in dreams I go
to fly through the windows and doors of my soul
again I awake
praying my soul to save
what is my demise
I search for answers through childlike eyes
to what end do I go
to the bitter end I am told
so many roads I have traveled
hopeless dreams crushed, left to unravel
though I feel I have fought hard and long
my heart weak, yet beats strong
low in the deepest depths of my memory
is the love you placed inside of me
my soul is growing tired
my thoughts more uninspired
with hopes and dreams of what used to be
please come set my soul free.
till then I will keep defying destiny.

Thanks

Thanks for all the time
to help me process and clear my mind
of what was keeping me here
of lost life
I ha e missed so dear
but now I find
I want back my mind
with you my dear
I see it slowly disappear
so I must say to you this day
I know who you are and why you came
but instead
I will redeem my soul and soon I will let
go of all the things that had me bound
letting the love of myself be found
trust is in motion here
only to myself do endear
for I know what it is to be lost and then found
now I will be ready for my crown
I have broken free from life and all its iniquity
I can finally say
I have found freedom anyway.
So, I say to all of you that are ones in hope
may our memories quickly invoke
healing upon our very souls
or with Satan you will go
life with our Savior is now at hand
God's mercy be with all of you
as death has no end
there is peace in my heart this very night
there is only peace in sight
and try, as you will
you will fail
the loved ones of God will prevail
To God we give our thanks.

Tomorrow

Let it be said my children
as I sit on my heavenly throne
I watch you constantly
you are never alone
even as the world turns and the ground shakes below you
fear not, angels will protect and guide you through
life is not a mystery as the door to a new world arrives
be at peace, all questions will be answered you have had locked
inside
now as you look to the beauty of this your new life
enjoy, relax, out of harm's way
I promised you this would happen some day
your mouths will be without words
your eyes will fill with tears
of joy not sorrow
while observing my rainbow promise
of everlasting life tomorrow.

New Dawn

The lights are out
another day is done
piercing lights of blue
come through my window with
such a heavenly hue
I have learned to let go
to feel love that I have never known
I possess from within
no matter how dark my paths, how dim
I think of paradise, how beautiful the view
it gives me hope and my strength is renewed
so one more day I can endure
no more wanting or needing, just resting assured
that I am one in myself with God now
in my place I do humbly vow
from tomorrow's new dawn
I will look far and beyond
this world and all its events
to keep focused on God
and await for the new dawn.

Time is Near

We are coming my friends
and we do intend
to show you where to go
a beam of light will shone
against the night skies
showing you the signs
we will show you the way
urging you to go without delay
the earth shall move
the water rise
but my children
will be safely hidden away inside
we bring peace, have no fear
God is coming, time is near.
(Written Oct. 98, after my dream of pandemonium)

Farwell

Deceivers of the light
follow me each and every night
not knowing who I could be
trying to capture the light inside of me
so come along
you will see who is really strong
follow me to the gates of hell
and there you will stay
as I bid you farewell.

Heaven's Gate

Heaven's gate is opening wide
to bring all God's children safely inside
as the passing days go quickly by
the nights seem eternal with no end in sight
the angels say, follow the light
filling us with love of the divine
helping us yet a steeper mountain to climb
they say the greater the mountain the less are our fears
with love we will Satan's scorn conquer
putting an end to each ones trembling and tears
the angels remind me of what path we must stay on
to capture the hearts of mankind
to relieve their hardest roads in life
I can see the road to heaven's gate
it is not so very far away
as God's heavenly trumpet sounds
we will stand on God's holy ground
safe and out of harm's way
we are entering heaven's gate.

Falling Star

A falling star fled across the sky
Of lavender, yellow and white
I felt the star was answering
some of my deepest questioning
I went into what seemed
like a strange but beautiful dream
I walked with Jesus for a time
He told me of future days and what I would find
I saw myself on a mountain top
then into the valley's we would go
He showed me things I did not know
times to come looked pretty grim
because man had so much greed and sin
oh, the pain I could see on his face
as he said, my people are such a disgrace
I asked how can I help,
what can I do
he said, it is too late
for so many of you

the mountains will crumble
the sea will roar
there will be nothing but greed filled wars
for my children that have not abandoned me
I will protect them on their journey
I saw the gates of heaven swing open wide
and all the beauty on the other side
angels were singing in such harmony
as they welcomed in you and me
I promise you my Lord
I will do
everything I can do to follow you
in one fleeting moment I awoke
thinking about the words
Jesus had spoken
If you have questions
no matter how near of far
the answers will come to be
when you see a falling star.

Rein in Peace

Cold, cold hearts
we are so very far apart
our lives are in such dismay
fighting endless battles day after day
as united we try to stand
we are left to sink in deep and shifting sand
trust, what is trust
where is the faith you placed in us
our heavenly father can you not see
life is not what we were taught it would be
or is this a new understanding, our true reality
we send our prayers in faith to you
hoping to receive answers to guide us through
all this caus and mess
answer our prayers, no more tests
as our awareness opens wide
now Jesus, we realize
you are one with us
no matter what unfolds, whatever our plight
we trust that you have us in your sight
and someday soon
you will say it is done
come be with me, we will rein in peace

Our Descent

The north has no solemn vow of presidency
the streets will be filled with grief
sin is in the forefront now
love is still the best choice of all
there is m:uch work to be done
from early mom till setting sun
put your lives memories to work of what you have known
follow the orders sent down from Gods throne
first the earthquakes
then the hurricanes and floods
massive power outages, looters and thugs
killing in the streets once filled with peace
safe places to go will be at an all time low
disastrous storms and unknown lights in the sky
leave our minds to wonder what is next and why
take heed my fellow man
lean only on God's commands
in times of trouble remember one thing
it is your soul God must redeem
in the last flickering moments you must repent
it is the only way to heaven and our promised descent.

Are You Ready

Are you ready for judgement day
you know it is coming, it is on its way
the good people of this earth have sinned and gotten greedy
all for me and nothing for the needy
how is it that they have forgotten to pray
asking forgiveness for their sins each day
Gabriel and Michael stand hand in hand
to warn the people across the land
change your ways before it is too late
why can't you love instead of hate
I wonder do you even care
challenge us if you dare
Gabriel will blow his horn
then what will you do
there will be no place to hide
that God cannot see you
God is calling, he is calling you today
for all of those who have gone astray
let go of all your worldly possessions
let go of your addictions and all your obsessions
there will be one taken and one left behind
will you be left behind because you were so blind
when the angels pour out their vials
then the earth will experience some horrible trials
the anti-Christ will have no forgiveness for anyone
what will you do then, with nowhere to run
wouldn't you rather change your ways
ask God's forgiveness and be on your way
to the promise land that has life without end
here comes Gabriel, so make up your mind
otherwise we will have to leave you behind
get ready my friends the day is coming
take a stand and make a difference
don't just keep slipping and falling
as they come to take us away
tell me now, are you ready.

Out of the Chill

A cold chill blows over the north
as zero waves hit our hearts
oh, beckon my soul that is quickly becoming numb
come give strength that I may fly
far from this earthly sky
watch for the millions of bright lights as they pass by
as they appear in the warm evening skies
we the angels of God's garden have plowed this earthly ground
and weeded as many souls as could be found
God is calling, to give us our wings
take heart my loved ones
soon your souls will once again sing
time is short as we know it now
watch for the horizontal rainbows appearing in the clouds
all your tears will finally be at an end
polish your being, we are about to descend
love is in the air
hear it calling from everywhere
be not dismayed what you see is real
soon your soul will be warm far away, out of the chill.

Time is Soon At Hand

Walk with me amongst the stars
then tell me who you really are
are you friend or are you foe
only God will know
you of the earth feel this is all there is
you die and that is it
would you believe there is a heaven
because there is
listen to me
try to start remembering
there was a time
when you could think of your destiny
before the clouds were hovering
put your minds at peace
for there is so much you do not know
put your memories to the te.st
and one day soon we will go
to that place where happiness did exist
you have read about it many times
it is a place so sublime
sometimes I take you there in dreams at night
so you can see a glimpse of what is in store
if you allow Jesus through your hearts door
someday you will come with him to the promise land
ask for his forgiveness and live your life right
you will be taken up on wings in flight
do not forget what I have said
the day is coming do not be misled
your planet earth
will take a turn for the worst
be ye not dismayed
you are living in the final days
with a blink of an eye
God will say it is done, it is time
there will be gatherings across the land
time as you know it is soon at hand.

Angels of Light

Oh, my little angels of light
working to save this earth day and night
I cherish your ways of love and healing
you pray for all with so much feeling
although your paths have been stressful and long
your love for everyone grows ever strong
I have not forgotten you and will hold true
my promise of happiness and endless skies of blue
you who have walked in so much pain
remember all those that you have saved
you are my chosen ones
roses from my garden of love
do not forget I am with you
I will deliver you to fly
far away from this earth
my precious angels of light.

Love

Create our passage to freedom
for your children on this earth
we have suffered much
can you still hear us
please God, please clear
all of our old ways and fear
place within our hearts a new song
we have trusted you for so long
please give us peace
and our long awaited release
you are our maker, with you there are no mistakes
we patiently wait for the clouds to break
let us walk amongst the stars
let our lights shine however near or far
your heavenly light surrounds us all
please do not allow us to fall
I say, love is with you this night
I will protect you with my ominous light
in dreams I will give you signs
to help save those hearts that are in decline
with each dawn comes a new reminder
I am with you always, I do care
faith be with you, you are never alone
until the day I come
to take you home
your reason for being here is love.

Satan Lets Go

How is it the world has come to be
everything other than God's philosophy
tainted ways
leaves us in such a haze
so, how do we get back to heaven's gate
how do we find God's pardon
for all the empty roads we have trodden
no time left to pray
no time left to think each day
what is God's chosen path
all we see are distorted maps
a little flicker of light here
a spark of hope there
let us gather in prayer
to regain our strength and our heavenly armor
and get ready to fight God's war
the angels will guide us and see us through
to fight this battle, our faith renew
as we are immersed in God's light
we become stronger
to win the fight
the orders have been given
from above
on Satan's ground we must trod
keep up the faith as we conquer the foe
we shall hear the sound of victory
as Satan lets go.

Open Door

The greener days are now at hand
no longer Satan singing victory with his band
the angels are healing his damage with much repair
a promise of love will be with you everywhere
follow your heart
it is never too late for a brand new start
walk into the fight
never let God out of your sight
in total amazement you will see
wondrous days await for you and me
all your tattered hopes and dreams
will be replaced with better things
let the past go
watch your heart grow
with love you can be sure
Gods plan will endure
take a stand just once more
walk with me through the open door.

Battles Won

There are times we feel in honor
there are times we feel distressed
over all our purest intents
where did our innocence go
now, it is the vaguest of memories
the dreams we thought would be
time is near an end
of what we know of our world
watch for angels that God sends
that will help to guide us home
to let us know we are not alone
tattered and torn our hearts may be
but we will be rewarded
for all our good deeds
strength for the troubadours will abound
we will fight until Satan has been brought down
so, Gabriel blow your horn
we will march to Jesus
and his majestic throne
we will bring down the walls of Jerusalem
now the battle has been won.

Last Call

Last call
in sight for all
where will we be
the last night in history
it is time of harvest
have we done our best
life is about change
a chance for all to rearrange
all of our possibilities
facing unknown realities
taking in stride
God is at the helm and by our side
whatever roads we have traveled
time is now to understand and unravel
all that was before us, leave behind, close the door
all that remains
should be Gods path to attain
sudden good-byes
are no surprise
all is in motion
without reason or slightest notion
now, let us stop and think
will we float of will we sink
climb to your destiny
freedom is waiting for you and me
grasp hold now, and you will not fall
God has given us our last call.

Wind Song

Wind songs come flowing from our universal skies
telling of a change drawing nigh
wind songs whisper while we dream
and take us to futures unforeseen
beyond those great midnight skies
do not be afraid to close your eyes to see
what lies beyond your dreams
wind chants will fill your head
telling us not to be misled
wind songs are getting stronger now
vibrations in your ears become noticeably loud
we are waiting for a sign
to take you to a newer dimension and time
to define all your dreams
to help explain what they truly mean
what is your true path and reality
in wind song dreams you will see
your minds open to full capacity
try to grasp hold, know the truth
the knowledge is there for the taking for all of you
it will be revealed where you belong
keep listening to all the wind songs.

Victory Across the Land

Open the gates and let us in
where we will abide and there is no more sin
so many souls are tired now
of treading the earth and the fields we have plowed
send in your heavenly troops
allow your workers time to regroup
send down your eternal love
so we may fight the battles this earth seems to be made of
let your chimes ring
let the angels sing
we are marching to your beat
with you, there is no defeat
so onward we will go
give us your armor and protection bestow
against the evil of this world
so we may cast evil into the fire hurled
the day of redemption is now at hand
our work is almost done
as we see victory across this land.

I Am Jesus

I am he who was born in a manger
so many years ago
a light shone bright around me so that you would know
that I am to be your savior
meek and mild without favor
I am he who walked the dusty roads
with many a parable told
I talked with my disciples
and told them what was to come
that one day soon I would leave them
to be with my father in heaven
I am he who healed the sick
and made the blind to see
just so I would prove to you that it was really me
I am the one you doubted
the day the soldiers came
then when you were asked if you knew me thrice you denied me
just the same
I am the one that received a crown of thorns
you stood by and watched as they pierced me with the sword
I am the one who carried that heavy cross
up to calvary
I am the one that asked the Father as I hung upon that tree
Father please forgive them for they know not what they do
as I hung there suffering for the likes of you
I am the one they laid to rest in that empty tomb
then you went away, your life to be resumed
I am the one who rose upon that third day
as the angels came and rolled the stone away
how surprised you were
to see me standing there
I am the one who had to go but promised you one thing
someday soon I would come for you
when the bells of heaven ring
I am the one
I am Jesus.

www.ingramcontent.com/pod-product-compliance
Lightning Source LLC
Chambersburg PA
CBHW022008120526
44592CB00034B/737